AF083921

Fabulous Fables from India

 ADAPTED FROM THE ORIGINAL AMAR CHITRA KATHA COMICS!

First published in India in 2023 by HarperCollins Children's Books
An imprint of HarperCollins Publishers
4th Floor, Tower A, Building No. 10, Phase II, DLF Cyber City,
Gurugram, Haryana – 122002
www.harpercollins.co.in

6 8 10 9 7 5

Text © Amar Chitra Katha 2023
Illustrations © Amar Chitra Katha 2023

P-ISBN: 978-935-6990-04-3
E-ISBN: 978-935-6990-03-6

This is a work of fiction and all characters and incidents described in this book are the product of the author's imagination. Any resemblance to actual persons, living or dead, is entirely coincidental.

Vinitha asserts the moral right to be identified as the author of this work.

All rights reserved. No part of this publication may be reproduced, stored in a retrieval system, or transmitted, in any form or by any means, electronic, mechanical, photocopying, recording or otherwise, without the prior permission of the publishers.

Cover and inside illustrations: Based on the artwork in the original Amar Chitra Katha comics

Typeset in Baloo 13pt/ 16
by Ketan Tondwalkar

Printed and bound at Nutech Print Services - India

This book is printed on FSC® certified paper
which ensures responsible forest management.

FABULOUS FABLES FROM INDIA

Adapted from the original
Amar Chitra Katha comics

WRITTEN BY VINITHA

contents

The Annoying Ant	7
The Unwanted Guest	23
The Fearless Boy	41
The Ghost That Got Away	63
The Great Architect	91
The Unhappy Tiger	108

THE ANNOYING ANT

Everything was peaceful in the jungle. The animals and other creatures were happily going about their day. So were a line of ants walking through that jungle that morning. And they would have walked through, like the way a line of ants walked – in a straightish way – and gone about their business of gathering food, had it not been for one little ant.

Have you watched ants? If you have, you'll know that ants are very hardworking. Ants live in colonies and, except for baby ants, all ants have tasks to do. Ants are busy from morning to night and they take their assigned duties very seriously. So that day, when one ant stepped out of the line, right in the middle of a new forest, and folded his arms and stuck his nose in the air, all the other ants paused, puzzled. "Where are you going?" asked one worker ant to this ant.

"I am tired of walking and walking and working and working," said this fellow, his nose still in the air.

Right above them butterflies fluttered and large flowers, laden with nectar, bent low to say hello. A big earthworm smiled, as it wriggled downward making a hole. The ant took a deep breath of scented air and said firmly, "Look how happy everyone is here. I think I'll stay here."

"Are you sure?" the worker ant asked. After all, he would have to go back and report it.

The little ant's smile broadened as another butterfly flitted by prettily. "There are so many different creatures and there is something or the other happening here all the time. I already love it so much! I want to stay here instead of marching every day, in and out, in straight lines, doing the same thing over and over again. I am going to be so happy here!"

And so, the other ants went on their way and this ant remained.

Everyone in this jungle went about their business without bothering the ant. Was our friend, the little ant, happy? No. This ant was not quiet, and had an opinion about everything. No one here was interested in his opinions, but he gave them out, nevertheless.

"You are so big and bulky, Mr Elephant!" he said one day to a kind elephant. The elephant trumpeted quietly. Did the ant stop there? No. He went on, "And even worse than your huge, fat trunk is your thin, scrawny tail with scraggy hair! What's with the ugliness? It just doesn't make sense."

Elephants are clever. They know that body-shaming is a form of bullying and that it is best to ignore it. So he trumpeted quietly and pretended like he had not heard the ant.

Did that stop the ant? No.

This tiny little fellow, smaller than the toenail of the elephant he was heckling, went on. "Really Mr Elephant!" he mocked. "Is that all you can come up with? A hurrump! Is that looooong nose of yours robbing you of words?" Hooting at his own wit, the ant went on to imitate the elephant's hurrump. "Harrrrrruuuummppph! Ha ha ha!" went the ant. "Haaaaaarupppp! He he he!"

In the shade, after a large satisfying meal, Mr Tiger had gone off to snooze. The constant chitter-chatter of the ant and the soft harrumphing of the exasperated, but patient, elephant disturbed the tiger. He growled, "What is all the noise about? Don't you know I'm trying to rest? I had a tiring hunt last night."

Do you think the growl would have had any effect on the silly ant? Of course not.

Turning his head, he spotted the tiger well-hidden in the tall grass. "Oh ho, Mr Tiger!" he hollered. "What happened? Did black paint run down your skin?"

Thank goodness Mr Tiger had hunted and eaten well because all he did was turn his angry eyes at Mr Elephant, who continued ignoring the ant and was quietly chewing on the leaves of a young tree.

Mr Tiger asked Mr Elephant, "Is this your friend, Elephant? Tell him to be quiet or I will."

A monkey who had been swinging from one mango tree to another, dropped down to hiss at the ant. "Watch it, Ant," Mr Monkey warned. "Don't tease the tiger."

"Or what?" asked the ant. He stood on his hind legs and shrugged his forelegs nonchalantly. "What, Mr Monkey? Tell me! What will he do if I tease him more? Will he squash me and add me as a dot on his skin? If he does that, who will he be? A tiger or a leopard? Tell me, tell me!"

And once again, the ant laughed at his own humour. He was really loving it here. The monkey stared at the brazen ant in horror. The ant looked at the monkey more closely and chuckled. He asked, "What's wrong with you, Monkey? Do you know how funny you look with your beady eyes and your wrinkled face?"

The monkey was angry now. "You horrid thing!" the monkey said, shaking his fists at the ant. "I should toss you over the trees, far far away, where nobody can find you."

The ant retorted, "With what will you toss me? With that ridiculous tail of yours?" He laughed loudly at his own joke. "You too have no proportion at all!" he added.

A peacock nearby overheard the exchange. Vain as ever, he didn't want to leave an opportunity for someone to praise him. He stood up proudly, fanned out his beautiful tail, and said rather smugly, "Look at me! Beauty, proportions! I have it all!" And the peacock danced.

Now, when a peacock dances, fanning his long, glorious feathers, the whole jungle watches in awe.

Not the ant. "Proportion?" hooted the ant. "What proportion? That ridiculously long tail of yours? As for the colours? Ha ha ha! Is that what you call beauty? Well, sweet sir, you couldn't be more mistaken! You are a mess of colours. Looking at them one wonders how confused you were! It feels as if you weren't sure whether you wanted a purple, a green or a blue! What did you really want, sir?"

Astounded because he was not used to anything but admiration, the peacock stopped dancing and fanning his beautiful feathers. "You!" he screeched. "I'll get you, you pipsqueak." With that he got ready to chase the ant.

The elephant stretched his trunk and calmed the peacock. "Relax Mr Peacock," said Mr Elephant. "Ant just talks too much. You ..."

Before the elephant could say another word, the ant cut in. "Oh! How lovely to hear you, Mr Elephant," he said. "At last you found your voice! I was beginning to think you had swallowed your vocal cords or your flappy, silly ears had blown them away!"

The elephant quietly looked at the little ant. He said, "You know, it is hurtful to say such things."

But the elephant's patience and kindness was wasted on the ant. He chortled, saying, "Hurtful? How can anything hurt you through that thick, hanging skin?"

By this time, the whole jungle had stopped to listen to the silly ant.

Mr Snake couldn't care less about all the conversation. He went slithering by looking for a patch of sun, ignoring the group.

Mr Ant, on a good wicket with making fun of everyone, immediately said, "Hey! Look at that funny thing! It doesn't even have legs. What can it do in this world?"

Mr Snake stopped in his tracks, expanded his hood and hissed. "When I sink my fangs into you, you will know what I can do!"

But did that keep Mr Ant quiet? No. "You think your silly fangs can find a way to get into my lovely little body!?" jabbered the ant. "What a hoot you are! Ha ha ha!"

Now all the animals were angry. They all glared at the ant. "What?" demanded the belligerent ant of Mr Elephant who seemed really upset now. "You are scared of that ... that ... legless thing? Can't you use those great blocky feet of yours to stamp him?"

The elephant realized that nothing – certainly not kindness – would keep the ant quiet. The ant, the elephant decided, needed to be taught a lesson. "I have been really patient with you," he said. "But now you need to stop talking."

"Or what?" asked the ant, full of himself. He charged up to the elephant to holler at him and teach him a few lessons, as well. "Who do you think you are? What do you think you will do if I

don't stop talking? Huh? You are tooooo big and tooooo slow to run, and tooooo stupid to think and tooooo old to ...!"

The ant abruptly stopped the jeering. The elephant was moving through the jungle, and moving rather swiftly. "Hey hey HEY! What are you doing? Where are you going? Not so fast! Put me down! Heeeeyyyyyyy!"

"Didn't you just say I was slow?" asked the elephant, striding through the jungle. He was heading to the pond in the middle of the jungle. In two long strides and way before the ant could scamper down, the elephant was in the water.

"HEYYYYY!" screamed the ant, in complete panic. "What are you doing! Where are you going? I hate water!"

"Oh, Challenger of Elephants and Tigers and Snakes!" said the elephant who was calmly treading the water and going deeper still. "Don't tell me you are afraid of a little water!"

Elephants are great swimmers and love playing in the water. Mr Elephant splashed around and went deeper. Now his entire body was in the water and only the top of his head showed over the surface of the water. The ant looked in horror as the water rose all around him. When Mr Elephant splashed around, the ant leapt as large droplets of water fell around him. "Take me back, take me back! Get me to land AT ONCE!"

Mr Elephant ignored the ant, just the way the ant had ignored him and everyone else in the jungle. The water lapped at the feet of the ant

and now the ant was in tears. "Take me back to land!" he cried. "I'll get swept away! I'll drown! Heeeellllpppp! Please!"

"I think that will be the best for everyone if you do get swept away," said Mr Elephant. "You certainly won't be missed. In fact, we'll all be happy. No more nasty comments, no more making fun of anyone else."

"I'm sorry, I'm sorry," wept the ant. And he really was. "I won't say another word about anyone! I promise!"

The elephant smiled to himself and raised his head a little more. He knew he had to right this wrong, properly. "Will you apologize to everyone whose feelings you've hurt?"

"Yes, yes, yes!" said the ant fervently. And he really meant it. "I'll do everything you say. Just get me out of the water. Please!"

The elephant smiled. He swam to the bank of the pond and then waded out of it. As soon as he was sure that the elephant was safely on land, the ant scrambled down and scurried to the floor of the jungle. He kissed the earth, rolled on the ground and said, "Sorry, sorry. No more teasing. No more, I promise. I'll go about my work with my family and mind my own business."

He meant it. The elephant and all the animals in the jungle knew that. They all went about their lives, as did the ant.

THE UNWANTED GUEST

In a small kitchen of a small house in a small village of Arakatavemula in Andhra Pradesh, Buddhimati inspected her larder and saw what she already knew. There was not a single lentil to cook that day.

Her husband, Vishnu Rao, was a priest. He barely earned enough money for his family to get by.

When she checked the rice jar there was a handful of grains and she sighed in relief.

Buddhimati, like most women in their kitchen, knew how to stretch the little that they had. She made it look like it was easy to do so. But Buddhimati had been doing this now for so many years that it was starting to take a toll on her.

She scraped all the grains of rice in the jar and thought hard. There was just about enough for her to put together a Pulihora (tamarind rice).

Buddhimati started to make it. She washed and soaked the rice and set it to boil, while she took a small ball of tamarind and soaked it. As the rice fluffed out, she chopped ginger, gathered fragrant spices and crushed them. She picked a single grain of rice to see if the salt and tanginess was right. It was. Her stomach rumbled. "I hope I get to eat some of this," she thought, as she added a bit more salt and sprinkled in the crushed spices and turmeric.

But even mid-thought, Buddhimati knew that she probably would not get even a morsel to eat. Vishnu Rao, her husband, had a habit of inviting anyone who was at the temple at noon, to his home. "I'm sure my dear husband will bring another guest home today as well," thought Buddhimati, glumly.

Just as she had predicted, Vishnu Rao reached home for lunch with a man.

"Ah, Buddhimati," said the priest, "a guest has honoured us again today. Will you set one more plate for my friend here?" Standing next to him the villager bowed and beamed. Buddhimati bowed and did what one did when a guest

came in. She welcomed him, and left to clean one more space, and lay another leaf for lunch.

Buddhimati suspected that everyone in the village was aware of her husband's generosity and was taking advantage of it. The guest smiled as he rinsed his hands and sat down to eat. The guest and her husband sprinkled a little water on the banana leaf that had been placed in front of them. Buddhimati then served them the fragrant, delicious Pulihora that she had made with the last few fistfuls of rice.

Both men ate and appreciated the food. Buddhimati really did cook a delicious meal.

Buddhimati smiled sadly to herself when the guest said, "This Pulihora is delicious. May I have another serving?"

Vishnu Rao smiled proudly and said heartily, "Of course, of course!"

As soon as the guest left, Buddhimati allowed the tears that she had held back to flow. But one more day of eating nearly nothing made her angry.

"Why must you bring people home every single day?" she shouted. "Do you know that our children have not eaten anything since yesterday?"

Vishnu Rao, belly filled, said, "We must put the needs of others before our own, Buddhimati."

"Can't you see that these people are taking advantage of you?" Buddhimati asked, exasperated.

They had been having conversations like this daily now. But no matter how much she reasoned with her husband, he remained adamant.

"I won't hear another word of this," he said.

And he wouldn't.

Day after day, Vishnu Rao continued to bring people home. He'd urge anyone who reached the temple by noon time or anyone he met on his way from the temple to his home, to join him for lunch. And of course, they did.

He never enquired about what his children ate or whether they ate at all. Every day Buddhimati and the kids would eat scrapings from the

bottom of the bowl, and drink water to fill their stomachs. When this kept happening again and again, Buddhimati realized that nothing she said made a difference to her husband.

One afternoon, after cleaning up the kitchen and after comforting her hungry children to sleep, Buddhimati decided to take matters into her own hands. She came up with an idea that put a smile on her face. It was a good idea and Buddhimati knew she had to give it a shot. Things just couldn't continue as they were.

The next day, as usual, at noon, her husband walked into their home with a guest.

"Buddhimati!" he announced brightly, "Look how wonderful the Lord is. He sent us a guest. Please set one more plate for food."

Buddhimati was ready. "Welcome, welcome!" she said with a warm smile.

Vishnu Rao was taken aback. His wife seemed happy! The guest of course smiled back.

"Is lunch ready Buddhimati?" Vishnu politely enquired, smiling.

He felt slightly uneasy, seeing his usually grumpy wife so cheerful today. In fact, it seemed as if she was prepared for a guest. Buddhimati was cleaning the area where she served food to her husband, to make place for their guest.

"Yes," she answered without turning around, with a quiet smile to herself. "I have made some Gongura pachadi and Aavakai (mango) pickle. You can eat it as soon as you have bathed."

"This is turning out to be a lovely day," thought Vishnu.

Gongura pachadi, made of sour sorrel leaves, eaten with hot rice, was his absolute favourite.

Vishnu was extremely pleased. His wife had been quarrelsome for so long that seeing her smiling and cleaning the kitchen so timidly lifted his heart. "The Lord is amazing," thought Vishnu Rao. "He has made this good woman realize that god is in a guest."

Relieved that there would not be an argument as soon as the guest left, and certainly not interested in doing anything to alter Buddhimati's mood, he didn't even wonder why his wife had asked him to bathe. He joyfully said, "Okay! I'll head off to the river to bathe. I will be back soon."

And with that, he trotted off.

Once he was out of the way, Buddhimati turned to the guest, who had seated himself comfortably in front of the leaf on which food would be served.

"Are you comfortable?" Buddhimati asked the man. He had washed his hands and was ready to eat as soon as his host, the priest, returned.

"Yes, yes," said the man, smiling broadly.

He was licking his lips in anticipation of the fluffy, steamed rice and the hot Gongura pachadi with a dollop of mango pickle, that had been promised. Knowing that the food would be served as soon as Vishnu returned from his bath, the man was waiting patiently.

"I have heard such wonderful things about the food you cook," he added.

Smiling, Buddhimati turned around and brought out a stout stick used to pound chillies and spices. Without glancing at her guest, but fully aware that he was watching her, she gently placed the stout stick against the wall in the corner of the room. She then went to the kitchen and taking a ladle and a brass plate she banged them together for a bit. She did this all while completely ignoring the guest. Then she came out of the kitchen holding a thali with a lamp, a garland, kumkum and sandal paste.

Devoutly Buddhimati went to the stick and started worshipping it. She chanted under her breath, applied the kumkum on the stick, brought the lamp close to it and then after bowing low three times, placed the garland

on the stick, with complete reverence. Then she chanted loudly, eyes shut. When she heard a scrambling sound and a throat clearing, Buddhimati smiled inwardly. But she didn't show it. She kept her eyes shut and continued chanting loudly.

"Ahem!" said the man. He was so curious, he could not bear it any longer.

"Hush now!" said Buddhimati. "Don't interrupt my pooja."

Knowing that her husband would be back in another five minutes, Buddhimati pressed her head to the ground and threw some flower petals on the stick. Without glancing back, she hoped that she had done enough to gain the full attention of the guest. Then she turned around and said, "I'm sorry, I have to do this. This is an important ritual in my home, nowadays."

"Worshipping a stick?" asked the guest in wonder. He considered himself a well-travelled man and he was sure he had never seen or heard of sticks being worshipped. "What for?"

"Oh, every time my husband gets someone home for a meal, I perform this pooja," she replied.

The guest was even more puzzled. A stick pooja when guests come? This was unheard of!

"You see, I believe that if I purify the stick in this way, then the gods will forgive my husband," added Buddhimati.

"Forgive your husband?" questioned the man, with growing alarm. "Why?"

"Don't you know?" asked Buddhimati, looking at him with wide-eyed innocence. "After feeding the guest well, my husband beats the guest well. If I do this pooja properly, I know the gods will forgive my husband."

The man stood up, alarmed. "What!" he exclaimed, in terror.

"Yes," said Buddhimati. "My husband has gone crazy. But I don't think you need to worry," she added reassuringly to the man who was already hastily walking to the door, his eyes fixed on the stout stick that was leaning against the wall. "My husband seems to like you. I don't think he will beat you hard."

Her last words were barely heard, as the man hurriedly slipped his feet into his slippers and walked out briskly.

"Wait!" shouted Buddhimati to the fleeing figure. "What will I tell my husband?"

"I just remembered I have to leave immediately!" shouted the man, increasing his pace. "I need to feed my cat!"

Then, seeing Vishnu Rao in the distance, returning from the river, still wet from his bath – the man ran.

Puzzled, Vishnu hurried to his wife who was standing at the door with a stick in her hand. "What happened? Why is our guest running away?"

"He kept asking me to give him this stick and he got angry when I refused to give it to him," said Buddhimati.

"Why didn't you give it to him?" asked Vishnu Rao. "He is a guest in our house."

Grabbing the stick, Vishnu ran after the guest. "Wait," he hollered, shaking the stick in his hand. "Wait, sir!"

The guest turned around and saw the priest chasing him with a stick. He really couldn't believe his eyes. "Oh no!" he thought. "It is true. The priest has really gone mad. He is going to beat me, without even feeding me!" And the man ran for his life.

Vishnu chased the guest, stick in hand, puzzled. "Take, take, take!" he shouted. He pursued the guest as far as he could.

When the guest finally escaped, he told everyone about Vishnu Rao.

"His eyes were wide and he looked demented. He ran and ran, hissing and shouting to beat me with that stout stick. The faster I ran, the faster he ran! He was shouting and threatening and waving the stick! I saw it with my own eyes!" he said to anyone who would listen to him.

From that day on, Buddhimati never had to worry about unwanted guests at her home.

THE FEARLESS BOY

Samkicca was a novice – a young boy and a monk-in-training – who lived in a small community of monks. The monks had established a secluded monastery, on the outskirts of a small town, at the edge of the forest. After their austerities and meditation, Samkicca and the monks would head to the town and beg for food. Whatever each of them collected would be taken back to the monastery, where the food was divided equally and eaten.

One day, as they were about to eat, Samkicca looked up and saw an old man watching them. He looked hungry and tired. "Reverend, we have a guest," Samkicca said to the chief monk, who was eating his food with awareness.

Looking at the dust-covered man, the chief monk asked, "Where do you come from, brother?"

"A distant place, sir," answered the man. "I am on my way to my elder daughter's house. I was staying with my younger daughter, but she has fallen on hard times ..." The man let his sentence trail with a distant look of sadness in his eyes. After a pause, he added, "... and I had to leave."

"You appear to be hungry," the monk said kindly, adding, "eat with us."

Since the monks were already seated and since the food had already been divided equally, the head priest told the old man, "Go get a banana leaf and each of us will give you a portion of rice."

The man hurriedly did as he was directed and soon he was tucking into a hot, delicious meal. The food was wonderful. Even in the best of times the

man had not feasted this well. When he had eaten enough, and enjoyed every morsel of the meal, he turned to the monks, quite sure that this kind of abundance was not a regular thing. "Reverend, have you come from a feast?"

"No, brother," answered the monk. "We have not."

Guessing why the old man may have thought so, Samkicca added, "This is the kind of food we collect every day."

The other monks nodded, while the chief monk averred, "The people here are good to us."

Amazed at the rich food he had eaten – the clarified buttery rice, the kheer, and lentils and the vegetables – the man thought to himself, "I could never hope to get food like this even if I work every day from dusk to dawn."

He gauged his situation – he had never eaten a meal at his daughter's place. He was heading to live with another daughter but who knew what her means were and even if he worked all day … He quickly did some mental calculation and blurted out, "Reverend, I would like to live with you."

When the monks went quiet, the old man pleaded, "I shall perform any task you assign me."

"Very well, you may stay with us," the chief monk agreed, nodding.

No further questions were asked and the man happily settled in the monastery. However, a few weeks after eating comfortably and doing the little he was asked to do, the man grew restless.

"How I long to see my daughter," he thought to himself. The bare walls of the austere monastery, the silence in which the monks meditated, the distance from his daughters, all troubled him. In his head, he heard his grandchildren laugh, and saw them pattering about, cuddling with him and begging for stories. All of that now felt so far away and so precious.

He felt a great urge to see his grandchildren. "Will the monks give me permission?" he wondered. Detachment from the material world is what monks practised. After living with them he was sure they would not approve his need to see his family. Imagining a refusal from the monks, the old man's thoughts grew even more rebellious. "Why do I even have to ask anyone for permission to see my family?"

So, just before dawn, the man collected his things and quietly left the monastery. Carrying the small bundle of his meagre belongings, he headed to the forest through which he would reach his daughter's village.

He walked and walked until he was half-way into the forest. Suddenly a group of tall, fierce-looking men, carrying spears, emerged from the shadow of the trees. The man froze in shock. No one needed to tell him who these men were. "Robbers!" he thought in panic. He turned around to flee, but there was nowhere to go. He was surrounded.

The robbers were tall, their torsos bare and their heads covered with bandanas. They each held sharp-looking spears that glinted even in the low forest light. They had amulets tied to their arms and twirled their thick moustaches, their faces impassive. These men obviously meant business.

The man stood rooted to the spot, blubbering, as one of the men – the tallest, the fiercest-looking – peeled out of the group and walked towards him. The rest of the men closed in.

Falling to his knees the man held his tiny bundle aloft in surrender. "I don't have anything of value," he whimpered. "See for yourself!"

The robbers had been having a dry spell. The man, they could see, was poor. His ragged bundle didn't even need to be examined. The robbers seethed that once again, instead of accosting a fat, rich merchant carrying gold or goods, they had caught a poor, old man. Instead of letting him go, they trussed and dragged the man deeper into the forest where a space had been cleared off trees and undergrowth.

At the centre was an oblong boulder that had been garlanded. A chopped tree stump stood there. The

robbers hauled up the quaking old man and tied him to the trunk.

The leader of the robbers walked around the old man, twirling his moustache and considering his options. "The forest spirit has to be appeased!" he declared. "A human sacrifice! That is what will placate the gods!"

"Nooooo!" screamed the old man, in terror. There he was thinking of playing with his grandchildren and instead ...

Without further ado, and ignoring the man's tears and protests, the robbers untied him and dragged him to a chopping board. The man blubbered and wept and pleaded, but the robbers were firm. They were used to whimpering men. They had been unsuccessful for a while and it was obvious to them that the gods had to be appeased. This drought in their profession had to end.

When he realized that his pleas and tears were not moving the robbers to mercy, the man lamented aloud, "A wretch like me would make a poor sacrifice. Even the spirit would be offended."

When the leader, poised in the act of swinging his axe, hesitated, the man pressed forth. "There is a monastery, not far from here, where thirty men of noble birth dwell. Instead of making an offering of an old, wretched man like me, offer one of those monks instead. Can you imagine how pleased the gods would be with an offering like this?"

Now the leader was fully attentive and thoughtful. "Hmm. He is right," he said.

Turning to his henchmen he said, "Untie the wretched fellow."

Not believing his luck the old man joyfully said, "I will forever be indebted to you. If you ever need any help ..."

Before he could gush some more, the leader interrupted him. "I do," he said. "Lead us to the monastery."

"Cer ... cer ... certainly, certainly," stammered the old man.

'Start walking," snarled the leader, shoving him, "and don't even think of escaping."

The old man led the band of robbers to the quiet stone-carved monastery, well-hidden at the beginning of the forest.

Nothing stirred in the monastery and the leader was instantly wary. "I don't see any monks here," he said.

"They are in their cells," the old man explained. He knew their routine. "Sound the gong and they will come out."

The leader sounded the gong and one by one all the monks stepped out of their cellars.

"Who are you?" the chief monk asked, adding, "... and why did you ring the gong?"

"We are a gang of robbers who dwell in the forest," the leader said. "The forest spirit has to be appeased with an offering of human sacrifice. We have come to choose a worthy victim."

The monks listened to the robbers calmly. If the monks noticed that cowering in the midst of the robbers was the very man they had sheltered and shared food with and who, it was obvious, had led the robbers to their monastery, they said nothing. If they had any more questions, none were worded, either. Instead, without hesitation, the chief monk said, "Take me."

Immediately another monk said, "No, Reverend, we cannot spare you." Turning to the robber chief he begged, "Take me, instead."

"No!" said another monk in quick succession. "Please sir, take me."

And with that, each monk stepped forward, earnestly insisting, "Take me! Please, please, take me."

The robbers were astonished. They had encountered different people in their lives; soldiers and kings even. Never had they thought that this kind of bravery could be found in a monastery. The leader said with barely-

concealed admiration, "They are all brave men!" The old man, who had cowardly proposed their lives instead of his, eagerly wanted to take credit for this as well. He said dismissively, "They are brave because they have no attachment. I too would have been brave had I no daughters or grandchildren, or ..."

Disgusted, the leader roared, "Depart from my sight, you wretched man!"

Sighing in relief, the old man ran away from the robbers, thanking his lucky stars.

The leader now really had a challenge at hand. He still wanted to make an offering to his gods, but he only needed one human for this. He did not want to kill the chief monk, so he said, "I will take the youngest among you."

Hearing that, a young monk came forward cheerfully. "That will be me," he said.

That's when Samkicca bustled out of the crowding monks. "You are mistaken, my brother."

Samkicca had come to the monastery as a young boy. The minute he presented himself, the chief monk found himself crying out his name.

"Samkicca!" he said., "You are but a novice."

"I am the youngest person here, Reverend," said Samkicca softly. "I shall go. Do not stop me, I entreat you."

So, Samkicca left quietly with the robbers, while the monks watched in silence.

The robbers led the young boy through the forest to the clearing where their god was worshipped. "Sit," the leader commanded.

Wordlessly Samkicca obeyed. He sat on the mounted space used for beheading and did what he was used to doing – he meditated. He immediately went into a deep trance.

The robbers, impressed by the young boy's calmness, scurried around, organizing all that they needed

for the sacrifice. For the first time their prey was not crying and begging. He also did not have to be trussed up. "He is saintly," the leader said, "he deserves a merciful death." He sent his deputy to find the sharpest sword and sharpened it further, till it gleamed with a wicked light.

Samkicca was oblivious to all of this. Deep in his mediation, he sat with a light shining from within, his back erect.

The leader lifted his sword and held it aloft. He wanted to measure his move. "I will dispatch him with one blow," he thought. Ready to go through with it, he called out to the gods, "Receive this sacrifice O great Spirit and shower thy blessings on us!" With that, he swiftly slashed his sword in one sweeping stroke and …

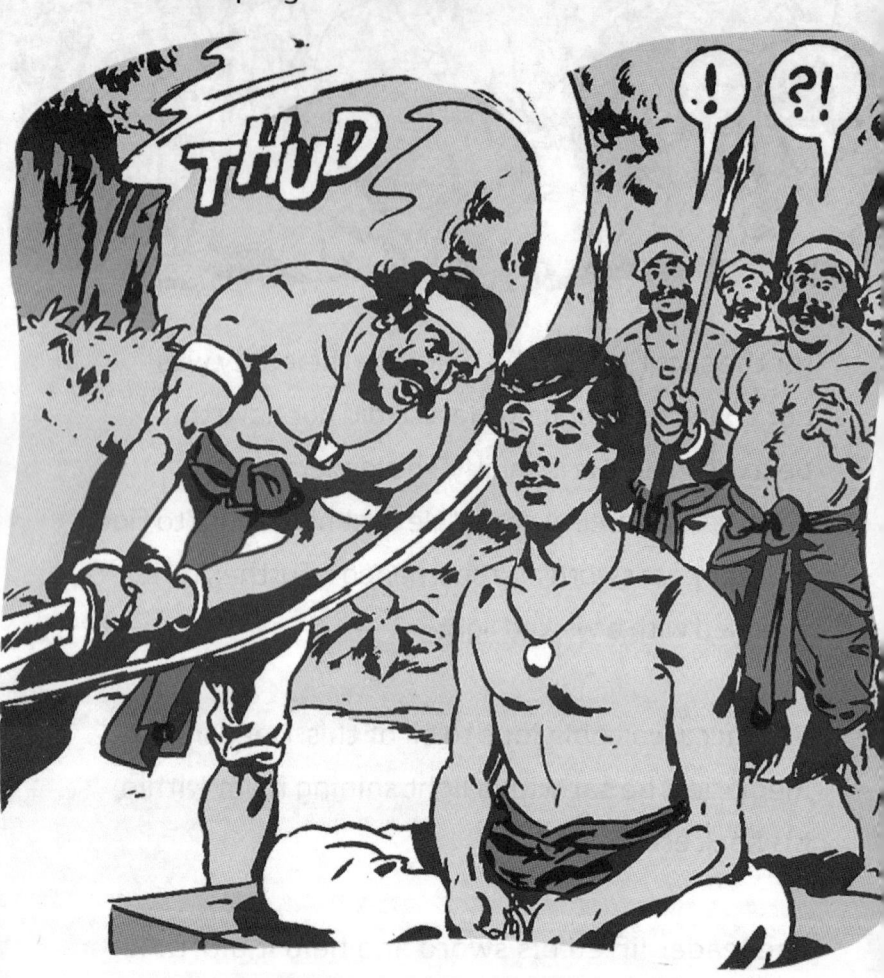

When he looked, he was astonished! The young boy was sitting straight as he had been all along, his head still intact. "Did I miss?" the robber wondered, startled. He was not one to miss anything. Yet, here was the boy sitting calmly. He had obviously miscalculated and had totally missed the boy. His band was watching him. "My hand slipped," he said.

He tightened his dhoti, wiped his palms and once again took position to chop the boy's head. He couldn't bear missing again, so he stood directly behind the boy this time. "This time I'll cleave his head in two!" he thought, as he lifted his hands high so that he could swing his sword with a lot of force.

The sword came down but the minute it touched the boy's head, it split in two. Samkicca continued to sit, unmoved. It seemed as though the sword had not even touched him.

The young boy was no ordinary mortal, the leader immediately realized.

"I have broken my sword on your head," he said to the boy. "Yet you remain so calm. Have you no fear?"

Samkicca came out of his trance. When he looked up, the band of tall, fierce men had gathered around him. Many of them were bowing in front of him.

"He that is free of desire has no mental suffering," he said. "To the one free of attachment, death holds no terror."

The clarity of his words, the brightness of his eyes, his lit face ... all this inspired the robbers. Their leader was on his knees. Hands joined

together, he said, "I shall give up my life of lawlessness and follow you."

"We will too, we will too!" chorused the rest of the robbers.

And that was how Samkicca, who had gone into the forest with a band of robbers, returned to the monastery with a band of disciples.

THE GHOST THAT GOT AWAY

Dhania, a young grocery store owner, lived in Kangra, a small village in Himachal Pradesh. Dhania's shop was small – and thank goodness for that – because had he a big business, god knows what would have happened to worrywart Dhania.

If customers paused too long over a sack of grain or if they examined anything in his store, Dhania would fret. "Is that a rotten tomato he's holding?"

he would wonder, nearly chewing all his nails in panic. "I'm sure they won't buy anything now."

Of course the vegetables and grain that were in his shop were fresh, and of course the customers would pause and look and decide. But Dhania was Dhania, and he would worry.

Dhania's wife, Devi, was from a nearby village. One day, he had to head to her village for a few days on business. When he told Devi this, she was happy. "That's wonderful," she said. "You can stay with my parents while you are there."

Dhania became nervous. "No, no!" he said immediately. "That's not necessary. I don't want to be a bother."

"Don't be silly," Devi smiled. "They will be happy to see you. I will send word to them at once."

And that was that, at least as far as Devi was concerned. Little did she know the anxiety roiling inside her shy husband.

Convinced that he would go there and make a fool of himself, Dhania barely slept that night. The next day, when Dhania met his childhood friend Kulfi Ram, the anxiety was clearly etched on his face. "Ah, Dhania you look nervous as ever!" said Kulfi teasingly. Kulfi was very fond of Dhania and knew that his friend became anxious over the smallest of things. "Has somebody asked you for rice on credit? Ha ha ha!"

Poor Dhania didn't find anything funny. He said, "Don't poke fun at me, Kulfi Ram. This time it is really serious."

"Is that so?" inquired Kulfi Ram, with a gentle smile. "Tell me, my friend, what happened? What worries you so?"

Shoulders bent, brow beaded with sweat, Dhania took a deep breath and said, "Well ... er ... I have to stay at my father-in-law's house for a few days. Without Devi."

Looking at his friend wringing his hands, Kulfi Ram who had expected much worse, burst out laughing. "Ha ha ha. Is that all?" he asked, relieved and also slightly puzzled. "What's there to worry? You should be happy! A son-in-law is always pampered. You will be too."

"This is the first time I am going there, without Devi," Dhania explained. "What will I talk to them about? I am very nervous."

"I have an idea! Why don't I come with you?" Kulfi suggested. "That way I can tell you exactly what to say and what to do."

Dhania was delighted. "Would you really do that for me?" he asked. "That would be perfect."

A few days later, the two men set off to the village where Dhania's in-laws resided. They chitchatted as they travelled, and time went by the way it does when two friends are together. As they came close to their destination, Dhania started to get nervous again. He really did not like making small talk with people and these were his wife's parents. If they stared at him and smiled, what would he say?

"Oh, Kulfi Ram," he said, "I am so nervous."

"Calm down, Dhania," said Kulfi Ram, soothingly.

"It is very simple. Are you worried about the kind of impression you will make on them?"

Dhania nodded his head vigorously.

"To make a good impression there are only two things you must do," Kulfi told him. "Firstly, make sure that you do not talk too much."

Dhania was impressed. He thought to himself, "Kulfi is right. I must keep quiet or they will think I am a chatterbox!"

Kulfi went on, "And second, make sure you do not eat too much."

Dhania was even more impressed. He thought to himself, "Oh, yes! Of course I must not gobble all the food that they place in front of me. They will think I am a glutton."

He looked at Kulfi Ram with adulation. "You are very smart Kulfi Ram!" he said.

Armed with these two gems of wisdom, Dhania felt less nervous. "Don't speak too much, don't eat too much," he kept chanting to himself as he walked forward. Easy peasy.

That evening, they reached Dhania's in-laws' home. The old couple were waiting for Dhania at the doorstep. "Namaste Jawai ji," they greeted Dhania as soon as he reached.

Dhania immediately responded with, "Namaste, namaste, how are y ..." and he stopped and bit his tongue, remembering how he must speak as little as possible.

The elderly couple smiled and welcomed Kulfi Ram too, ushering them into their home. "How was your journey?" inquired Dhania's mother-in-law. "Did you have anything to eat?"

Poor Dhania was in a fix. "Oh no!" he thought. "She is asking me! Should I answer? But if I answer, won't she think I am a blabbermouth?"

His in-laws waited for him to respond, with gentle smiles on their faces. Dhania was desperate. He really did not know what to do. Should he respond? Should he tell them he hadn't eaten? And if he did, would they think he was a greedy person? Poor Dhania looked desperately at Kulfi for inspiration, pleading silently for support.

Kulfi Ram quickly came to his aid. Bowing to his hosts, Kulfi said, "My friend here is just tired after the long journey. I think he would like to rest."

The hosts ushered the two young men in and urged them to wash their hands and faces and sit for dinner that had been prepared. Beautiful copper plates were placed for them and Dhania's mother-in-law started serving them hot and round puris.

The puris were golden and puffed. Dhania's mouth watered. After a long journey, the thought of hot puri and subzi made his stomach rumble.

He happily tore the puris and allowed the steamy, hot puris to melt in his mouth. In a minute he had finished all four puris that his mother-in-law had served him. Pleased, his father-in-law urged his wife to serve more puris to their young son-in-law saying, "Jawai ji is really hungry. Serve him some more puris, quickly."

"Of course!" said the woman, joyfully. She hurried and fried more puris and came to serve him saying, "Here, please have some more."

Dhania would have gobbled this lot of puris too, effortlessly, because he really was hungry, but even as he raised his arms to allow the puris into his plate, he remembered the second guideline that his friend had told him. "Oh no!" thought Dhania. "What have I done? I have gobbled up so many puris and this is exactly what Kulfi Ram had warned me not to do. Now my wife's parents will think I am a glutton! I must stop! I must not accept another morsel in my mouth!" Nearly sobbing because he really wanted to eat the delicious melt-in-the-mouth puris, he used his extended hands to indicate he was done.

Both his in-laws were puzzled. The young man who had just been eating with joy and gusto, was now abruptly shaking both hands over his plate, refusing food!

"Please have more puris!" urged the old man. The old woman bent to place them on his plate. Poor Dhania, his stomach still had so much

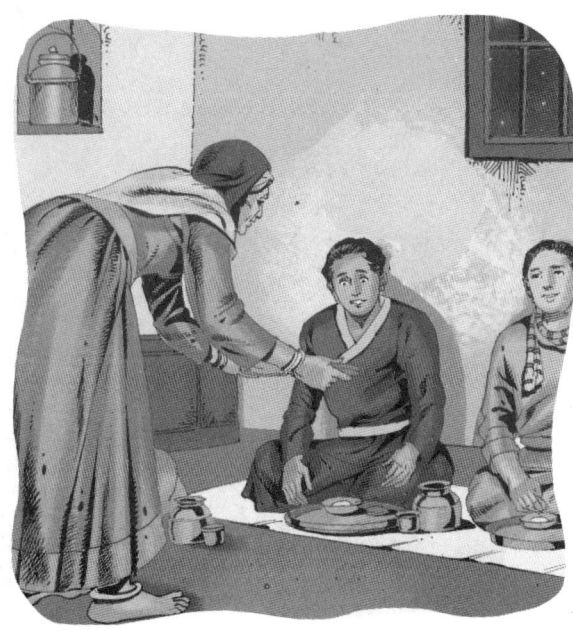

room for food, mutely kept shaking his head and waving his hands over the plate, indicating that he would not eat anymore.

Both the in-laws looked puzzled and Kulfi Ram once again intervened. "Oh, he has a small appetite," he said. "Don't worry, the food won't go waste. Please serve me his puris."

Later, beds were made and everyone turned in. But poor Dhania could not sleep. The thought of those puris and the emptiness of his rumbling

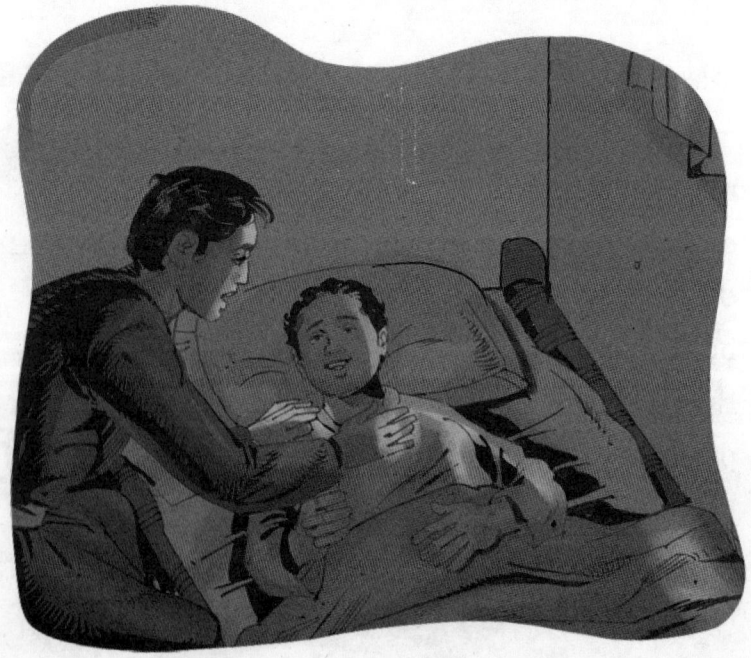

stomach made him miserable. He woke Kulfi Ram, who was sleeping contentedly next to him. "Wake up, Kulfi Ram! Wake up! I am starving. How can you sleep with all the growling sounds of my stomach?"

Kulfi woke up. "Huh! Starving! After that meal fit for a king, how could you be starving?"

"Yes, it was lavish, but did I eat? You tucked in, but you told me that to create a good impression I must not eat too much. So, how could I eat? I never got to savour this king's meal!"

Kulfi Ram was now fully awake and he understood his friend's hunger. "Dhania, everyone is asleep now. We will have to wake your mother-in-law and ask her for leftover puris."

"No way!" exclaimed Dhania. Waking his in-laws for food! "I'll never be able to show my face to my wife's folks again," he said.

Always full of ideas, Dhania came up with

another one. "Why don't we try sneaking into the storeroom outside?" he said. "I'm sure we will find some wonderful things to eat there." Dhania liked the idea and the two friends tiptoed out of their room and out of the house, and to the storeroom. But the storeroom had a huge padlock on the door. Dhania was so disappointed, he could have wept. His intrepid friend, once again, found the answer. Pointing at an open window in the storeroom, he said, "Climb on to my shoulders and jump into the storehouse from the window. I think it looks wide enough for you."

Dhania looked at the open window doubtfully. The main door was bolted and locked. "Once I am in, how will I climb out?" he asked. "I will get stuck inside. Imagine! And you will have to wake my in-laws to get me out. How does that make any sense? How will we explain why I am inside a locked storeroom, in the middle of the night? And even if I spend the night there, what will I tell them when they unlock the storeroom in the morning?"

"Slow down, Dhania!" Kulfi Ram said. "You always get ahead of yourself! I have a coil of rope. Tie it around your waist and get down through the window. I'll be holding the other end of the rope. When you are done eating, tug the rope and I will pull you out! Just as we did when we were children. Simple."

Dhania listened to what his friend had to say. "Hmmm, I suppose that could work ..." he said, sounding unsure. But any doubt he had was quickly quelled when his stomach again rumbled loudly in hunger.

Dhania took the rope and tied it around his waist. Then he climbed on Kulfi's back. Poor Kulfi grunted as he supported Dhania on his back, helping him reach up to the window. The buddy whom he had hefted all through his childhood, to steal mangoes from an orchard and for other mischief, was no longer a lad.

"Aaah, Dhania, you are so heavy!"

"Shhh!" hissed Dhania, as he hoisted himself over the open window and then ... jumped down.

He landed on his feet with a THUD and a loud, "OUCH!"

"Are you okay?" came the anxious voice of Kulfi on the other side. "I hope you haven't hurt yourself!"

"No, no! I am okay," answered Dhania in a hushed voice.

"Good. Now find something to eat, quickly."

The rope still tied to him, Dhania set out to explore the store room. He rummaged through different sacks, drums and large containers. There were grains, lentils, flour, chillies and other raw grocery items. Hungry and desperate, Dhania looked all around. He even rummaged inside small pots in cobwebby corners. Just then he looked up. High above, on the rafters of the inner roof, was a clay pot hanging from a rope.

"I wonder what that must be," he thought. "I bet it is full of honey or milk, and placed high to keep it safe from the cat!"

He immediately dragged a metal crate, and stood on it. But the pot was still out of reach. It was agonizingly close, but not enough for him to reach it. Dhania drooled and wrung his hands in agony. He looked around to see if there was anything he could use to grab the pot that he was now convinced was full of something delicious. He spotted a hefty stick. It gave him an idea. He took the stick and knocked the pot with it.

CRACK!

A steady stream of liquid began to slowly drip from the pot. Dhania opened his mouth and the golden liquid hit his tongue. It was honey! Dhania was delighted.

Just as he was enjoying the delicious nectar, the pot that had been hit by the stick gave way and

SLOSH!

— all the honey fell right on Dhania. He was splattered with honey, from head to toe.

"AAAARRGH!" gurgled Dhania in shock.

Outside, hearing his friend scream, Kulfi Ram panicked. "Be quiet!" he warned. "You will wake your in-laws."

Dhania was done with the adventure. "Kulfi Ram pull me out," he told his friend.

Just then, a light shone and much to Kulfi Ram's horror, Dhania's in-laws were there, holding a petromax lamp high, looking very alarmed. "What's that noise! Who is there!" shouted the father-in-law.

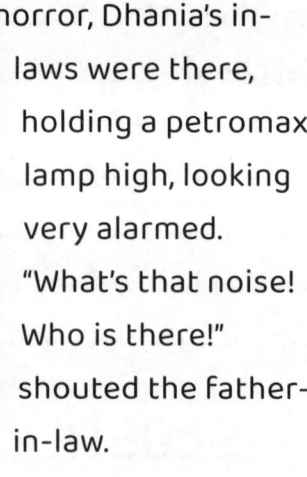

"Kulfi Ram! What are you doing here?" asked the mother-in-law.

Inside, Dhania heard the raised voice of his in-laws. He hid in a corner inside the storeroom, his heart racing. But outside, Kulfi Ram was quick to think on his feet. Looking as calm as possible he said, "I will tell you, but you must both promise to stay calm and not get too scared."

Nodding silently, they said, "Go on, what is it?"

"Well, you see, for about five years now, a ghost has been after me."

"A ghost!"

Gulping hard, Kulfi Ram proceeded. "Yes, a ghost," he said. "Unfortunately, it followed me here, to your house and got into the storeroom. I was trying to get rid of it, but I can't get in because the storeroom door is locked."

Dhania's mother-in-law and father-in-law were speechless. First to recover, the mother-in-law said, "Here, I have the keys with me. Let me open it."

This was exactly what Kulfi Ram was afraid of. He quickly said, "No, be careful. You must not let the ghost see you. Otherwise it will latch onto you and stay here forever."

Wide-eyed with anxiety, the father-in-law stammered, "Wh-wha-what can we do to help?"

"Give me the keys," said Kulfi glibly. "And hurry back to your room. Please hide, until I tell you that it's safe to come out."

The old couple hurried back to their bedroom and waited.

When he was sure that the old couple would not stir out of their room, Kulfi, keys in hand, unlocked the door of the store room.

Dhania, seeing it was his friend, peeled himself from the wall he had pressed into. "Ugh! Kulfi!" whispered Dhania. "Everything has gone wrong. Look at me! I am drenched in honey!"

Worried that the old couple may peep out from their room, Kulfi tried to hush his friend. But before he could say anything more, Dhania, sticky with all the honey all over him, tumbled out of the storeroom and into what he thought was their room for the night, saying, "I just need some fresh clothes!"

"Dhania!" hissed Kulfi Ram urgently, "... that is not ..."

Before he could get another word out, Dhania

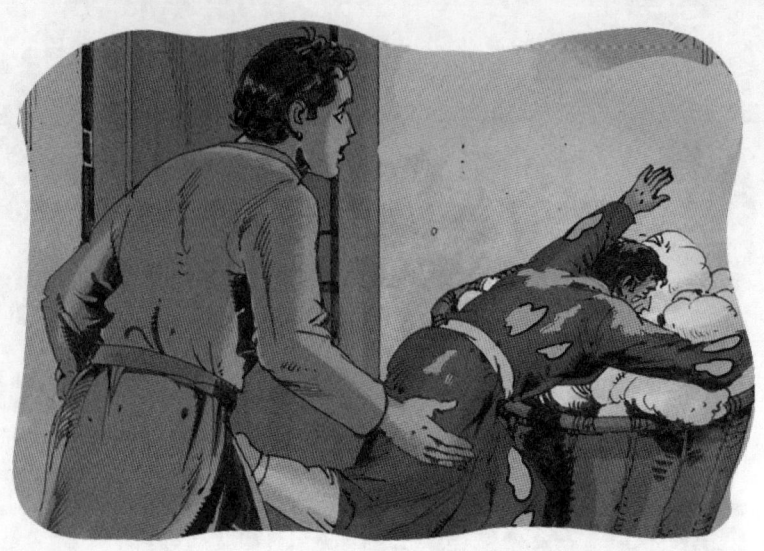

had walked into another room, and stumbled on a bale of freshly plucked cotton.

"AAAARGH!" shouted Dhania, already so frazzled by the turn of events.

Not too far away, two old people clutched each other tight, when they heard the crash and scream.

"What's that noise? Could that be the ghost inside our house?" asked the mother-in-law.

"I've no idea," quavered the man. "Let's take a peek."

When they peeped out, they really did tremble because outside a strange figure covered in misty white was running across their door. Hearts in their mouths,
eyes wide in terror, not needing to see anything more, the old couple shut their door with a crash, screaming, "It is the ghost!"

Dhania, who had been covered in cotton that stuck to him like glue because of the sticky honey, finally found his room. Kulfi Ram followed him.

"What am I going to do?" Dhania asked his friend, in despair. He had cotton covering his clothes, face, hair. The more he tried to pull the fluff off him, the more it stuck to other parts of him. He was a mess.

"You should wash up at the well behind the house," Kulfi whispered back. "Go. I will bring you your clothes."

So, Dhania tiptoed to the back of the house and peeled off his clothes. He dug a hole with a plough, and buried his clothes. Then using the pulley, he drew some water out of the well and

poured it on himself, feeling relief for the first time that day. By the time he washed his hair and body, Kulfi came with a towel and fresh clothes.

The two friends finally retired for the night.

The next morning, the two men woke up and got ready to leave. The old couple were up and Dhania's mother-in-law was already preparing delicious Babru. The two young men sat down for a hearty breakfast. Tucking into the delicious stuffed sweet black gram puris, paired with sweet tea, Dhania kept on saying, "Wah! This Babru is delicious. I'll have more." Pleased, his mother-in-law happily served him, thinking, "Oh, at least he has found his voice ... and his appetite!"

His father-in-law, however, was itching to say something. Finally, when they were nearly done with breakfast, the old man blurted out, "Did you manage to get rid of the ghost?"

"Oh, that ghost!" chimed in the old woman, her eyes round in fear, "I saw it with my own eyes!

Did you get rid of it?"

"Yes, yes, we chased it right out of here!" reassured Kulfi Ram. "Of course, I couldn't have done it without Dhania."

"Don't worry, it won't bother you again," added Dhania, reassuringly.

The old couple looked relieved. Before they could ask more questions, the two friends rose and took leave of their hosts. "We must get going," Dhania said. "I still have my business to attend to." They left with their bellies full of food and their hearts full of laughter.

"That ghost surely saved you last night, Dhania!" joked Kulfi Ram.

Circling his arm around his sweet friend, Dhania laughed in relief. "I tell you! I will never go back there unless that ghost is with me."

THE GREAT ARCHITECT

Prince Bodhi was enchanted with his new palace and was all praise for the architect. The fluted arches, the calligraphy on stone, the sculpture on the ceiling that seemed to move according to where one looked at it, the different durbars and rooms, each engraved with gems and lined with gold, stone curtains and polished wood … took everyone's breath away.

"I have never seen such splendour in stone!" the prince kept saying over and over again, as the architect who had been commissioned to create the new palace revealed his work. The prince was seeing the work for the first time and every inch was being scrutinized by him and his ministers. Not one of them could find fault with anything, yet.

The architect beamed with pleasure. He had indeed created many marvellous features in this new palace that he had never done before. He himself was very pleased with
the outcome.

"You have created a marvel!" the prince said, again. "Tell me, have you ever built a palace like this for anyone else?"

"No, Yuvraj," smiled the architect. "I have worked on so many projects, but I've never made anything like this for anyone else."

The prince was pleased. He was going to move into a palace that every king in the land would be talking about for ages! "Good!" he said, thrilled.

After the architect finished presenting the palace to the young prince and his entourage, he respectfully excused himself. He had some last minute work to delegate and some final touches to assign to his team.

As soon as the architect left, the prince, unable to contain his excitement, turned triumphantly to his friend and nobleman and said, "Did you hear that, Sanjikaputta?"

Sanjikaputta smiled in acknowledgement and said, "Yes, I did. This new palace of yours is unique."

Nodding with satisfaction, the prince said, "And I am going to see that it always remains so!"

Puzzled, Sanjikaputta asked, "How will you do that?"

Smiling, the prince said, almost to himself, "Oh, there are ways!"

Sanjikaputta immediately understood what the prince meant. With a sinking heart he thought to himself, "He means to slay the man whose creation it is!"

The prince had walked away and Sanjikaputta weighed his options. While the prince had not actually said anything, he knew exactly what the prince implied. Sanjikaputta felt sad that instead of being rewarded for the spectacular work he had done, the architect would in fact lose his life. "It would be a pity if one who possesses such talent were to be put to death," he thought.

This weighed heavily on Sanjikaputta's mind. A few days later, he went back to the site of the new palace and sought to meet with the architect alone. He would not be able to rest if he did not do the right thing and warn the architect of what might be his fate.

Recognizing that the nobleman in front of him was part of the entourage that had been there just a few days ago with the prince, the architect bowed low. "Have you finished working on the palace?" Sanjikaputta asked.

"Yes, my lord," answered the architect.

Looking straight into the architect's eyes, Sanjikaputta said, "Your talent is a sword at your throat."

Sanjikaputta saw the architect's eyes widen. He knew the clever man had received the implied message. Adding, "Be warned!" Sanjikaputta walked away hurriedly.

The next day, the prince summoned the architect to the palace. He wanted to set into motion his plan of ensuring that his brilliant new palace stayed a unique one. When the architect arrived, the prince asked him, "Have you finished your work on my palace?"

After Sanjikaputta's visit and his peculiar message, the architect had not slept the previous night. He had tossed and turned and thought of what the nobleman must have meant and of all the options he had before him. As soon as he was summoned by the prince, the architect understood that what the kind nobleman had warned him about was indeed true. He was prepared.

He smoothly said, "No, Yuvraj."

The prince was puzzled. To him it seemed that the palace was nearly ready to move into. In fact, hadn't the architect confirmed just that only a few days ago?

"What remains to be done?" the prince asked the architect.

"It is something that you haven't even dreamt of," said the architect.

The prince felt a surge of delight. Every single pillar and carving in the new palace was a marvel. To now be told that the cherry on the so-called cake — or the cardamom on the already delightful kheer — remained to be added, excited him. "It must be something incredible!" he thought to himself. He almost rubbed his palms with glee.

Before he could say anything, the architect spoke, "But right now I need some timber."

"What sort of timber?" asked the prince.

"Seasoned timber, with the sap well dried out, Yuvraj," the architect said.

It was not an unusual demand and so the prince said, "I shall have it sent to you." The prince dismissed the architect, but he stood there.

"Is there anything else?" asked the prince.

"Yes, Yuvraj," said the architect. "From now on I must work in absolute privacy."

"Oh!" said the prince.

"With the exception of my wife and son, no one should be permitted anywhere near the palace."

The prince was incredibly happy to hear this. In his mission to keep his palace design and architecture exclusive, this new turn of events fit in perfectly. The fewer the people in the know of the master plan of his exclusive palace, the better. Once this last design was put into place, then and only then would he finish off the architect. And lo and behold, his palace would be one of the wonders of the world! The only person who knew how to recreate it would have been executed.

The prince was thrilled. He joyfully said, "You shall have all the seclusion you need!"

Soon enough, beautiful, old, dry timber was delivered to the new palace. Once it arrived, all the staff in the architect's team, as well as all the staff from the prince's court, were despatched.

The architect shut himself in the courtyard of the new palace and started to work.

He had already drawn new plans. He now marked, sawed and chopped the wood to accurate measurements. He began a new complex task of building something he had never built before. This time he worked harder because his life depended on it.

Every afternoon his wife would walk to the new palace and the architect would let her in. She would bring him his meal and enough food for the night, collect the previous day's utensils and be there until her husband, the architect, ate his food.

They barely spoke. The architect was preoccupied with executing the design. He had no team to help him, so he was working doubly hard. To his wife, it seemed as though he was building a giant bird. She never asked any questions and the architect did not volunteer any explanations. He would eat his food and let her go.

After a few weeks, the different pieces were joined and flexed and fitted. The installation was nearly ready.

That very afternoon his wife did not come in at the usual time. When she finally arrived, she looked pale and worried. Before he could ask her why she was so late that day, his wife said, "Soldiers have surrounded the palace."

The architect sighed. He knew his time was nearly up. "The prince must be getting suspicious," he told his wife.

She looked at him wordlessly. The architect continued, "It doesn't matter now. Go home and sell everything of value in the house. When you come tomorrow, bring our son with you. Also bring all the gold we have."

With less than twelve hours to go, the architect worked twice as hard to finish his work.

The next morning, soon after dawn, there was the familiar knock on the door. When the architect cautiously opened it, he saw his wife. She had a bundle in one hand and their son in the other. She had done exactly as he had instructed. The architect hurriedly let them in through the new palace gate.

In the courtyard stood the final piece that the architect would ever make in this kingdom. It was a magnificent bird made of the lightest wood, its wings unfurled and ready to take off. The architect opened the door of the bird and gently deposited his son inside. With a step ladder ready by the door, he helped his wife inside. Then, muttering a quiet prayer that his latest creation would work, the architect entered the wooden bird.

He shut the door of the bird with his heart racing. He had calculated and double calculated; he had made a miniature bird and tried it out as well. But this was a giant version of a thing that had never been made before. With a final glance at the beautiful palace, he pulled the lever inside the bird. The architect hoped that he was right about this new but crucial invention of his.

As soon as the lever was pulled back, the giant bird, with the architect and his family in its belly, rose smoothly, and lifted off the courtyard. It rose high into the sky. The soldiers who had surrounded the new palace suddenly saw it clearly.

The army chief rushed straight to the prince. The prince had already suspected that the architect was building a secret weapon of sorts, inside his own palace – with his money and his materials. That was why he had asked the army to surround the palace, and bring the architect in. But nobody expected this.

"Yuvraj! It's not a weapon! The architect is trying to escape!" shouted the commander-in-chief, who had been ordered to wait for the prince's instructions.

"Shoot him down!" ordered the prince, furious.

The entire army trained their bows and arrows on the giant bird that was soaring and now turning left and making headway towards another kingdom. The archers took aim and fired.

Thud! Thud! Thud!

Some arrows met their mark and grazed the bird. But none of the arrows could stop the bird from flying off.

His heart light, as light as the beautiful creation he had made, the architect looked down. Below, as small as ants, were the soldiers still trying to shoot his bird down. He could hear the commander-in-chief bellow in rage, "He's escaped!"

What the prince said in response, the architect could not hear, because his giant bird was flying steadily in the direction he had charted out. In a few hours, the architect brought his bird down safely in another country.

There, the architect resumed his career. He built many, many marvellous palaces, each better than the last.

THE UNHAPPY TIGER

Rishi Muni, the sage, had just finished a havan and had settled down for his morning meditation when suddenly ...

Plop!

Something landed on his lap. When Rishi Muni looked down, he saw that it was a terrified-looking mouse. When he gazed up, the sage could see a few birds flying high up. Seeing the sage, one bird stopped circling and flew off.

"A mouse!" said Rishi Muni, holding the disoriented animal gently in his palm. "The eagle that was carrying it away must have dropped it, I suppose."

He gently opened his palm and allowed the mouse to scamper away saying, "Off you go, little one!" The mouse scrambled off happily.

In a little while the mouse returned to the sage, who was once again meditating. "Squeak!" he said, galloping as fast as his tiny legs could carry him, right back into the lap of his saviour.

When the sage looked up, close on the heels of the mouse, was the ashram cat.

Rishi Muni scolded the cat, "Go away! You are not to chase this mouse, you understand?" The poor cat screeched to a halt and, well reprimanded by the sage, slunk off. Rishi Muni picked up the mouse who sought refuge in him and was startled to find the mouse quivering.

"You are trembling!" he exclaimed. "You are frightened. You know the cat will come after you the moment my back is turned. You'll have to get used to being chased by cats, I'm afraid," he said.

"Unless …" Rishi Muni paused. His mind reconsidered what he was about to say. The yogi knew he could chant and do magical things if he wanted. He looked at the mouse and thought to himself, "Hmmm. Yes, I could do that!"

Glancing at the shivering mouse once again, the yogi took a decision. He lifted his hand and said a few words. And, lo and behold, the mouse turned into a cat!

The sage watched as the mouse examined his new version – his thicker tail, his retractable talons – and he purred. The mouse-cat went away and the sage did not see him for several days.

Then one evening, just as the yogi was returning from his evening dip in the nearby lake, he heard the growl and bark of an excited dog.

Before he could blink, a petrified cat dashed forward and took refuge between the folds of his dhoti. Right on its heels was the village dog, who now stopped short. The village dog stared at the yogi and turned away in a disgusted huff.

The cat pressed against his legs and Rishi Muni pursed his lips thoughtfully. "So now you are scared of dogs also, little one?" asked the yogi. He sighed and told the mouse-cat, "I can turn you into a dog as easily as I turned you into a cat, did you know that?" With that, Rishi Muni turned the mouse-cat into a dog.

The mouse-cat was now a fine-looking dog and the yogi was satisfied. "You make a handsome dog," he told the mouse-cat-dog. "Take care of yourself." The mouse-cat-dog went away happily, trying out his bark and his growl.

A few days later, when the yogi was busy choosing the right herbs for pooja, the mouse-cat-dog came galloping at full speed. Seeking the yogi, the mouse-cat-dog once again ran up to him, tail between his legs and hid between the yogi's dhoti, whining and howling, showing the whites of his eyes in fear.

The yogi scanned his surroundings to see what had turned the mouse-cat-dog into a jittery jelly. From the shadows of trees, a leopard emerged. The leopard, seeing the human, stalked off angrily and the mouse-cat-dog wilted in relief.

The yogi turned thoughtful. "Yes, a lot of dogs fall prey to leopards here," he said. "But I won't turn you into a leopard."

The mouse-cat-dog listened intently and looked hopefully at the yogi. After all, the yogi was his benevolent refuge and father figure.

Summoning all his energy the yogi shut his eyes and threw a spell on the mouse-cat-dog and ... Lo and behold! The mouse-cat-dog had turned into a ... Tiger!

"Tiger!" roared the yogi, "Now you need not fear ANYONE!"

The mouse-cat-dog-tiger, stretched himself to his fullest, threw back his head and roared with joy. The forest shook and grew quiet in response.

Soon, the mouse-cat-dog-tiger roamed the forest surrounding the ashram, enjoying his newfound freedom. Wherever he strutted, animals and other creatures rushed away. Just for fun, the mouse-cat-dog-tiger would roar loudly when he saw other animals run in terror. Life was good.

One day, while strutting around in the forest for fun and some snacks, the tiger saw two men hurrying on a narrow path, heading south.

The mouse-cat-dog-tiger grinned wickedly to himself and decided to have some fun. He had been seeing hares, and deer run away at his mere presence. It would now be such fun to watch humans scurrying away. He emerged from

the shadow of the trees, a low growl rumbling in his throat.

"T ... Tiger!" quaked one of the men, catching sight of the mouse-cat-dog-tiger. The mouse-cat-dog-tiger was about to growl and show his fine set of teeth to the men, when the other man calmly smiled and told the frightened man, "Don't be afraid. It is the ashram tiger!"

The other man was puzzled. Even the mouse-cat-dog-tiger paused to hear what the man meant by ashram tiger.

"Don't you know? It was originally a mouse," the man explained to the other man. "The sage transformed it into a tiger."

The frightened man now grinned, "Oh, I see!" he said. "A tiger with a mouse's heart, eh? Ha ha ha!" Laughing loudly, the two men ignored the big tiger and walked away.

The tiger soon found that even children considered him harmless. If he sauntered near any humans, instead of screaming and running away in terror, the little children smiled. Some even wanted to pet him. "It's the ashram tiger, silly," one little girl told her toddler brother. "He won't hurt us."

The mouse-cat-dog-tiger felt really insulted. "Even babies have absolutely no fear of me!" From being terrorized to terrorizing, the mouse-cat-dog-tiger had started to enjoy his life. Not being taken seriously was suddenly something he did not like, at all.

"A tiger who is not feared! This is an insult. I cannot tolerate this!" he thought.

When in trouble, the mouse-cat-dog-tiger usually went to the yogi and so his mind went straight there. "I will go to the sage and I will ask him ..." he thought to himself. That was when it hit him. He was a big tiger! He no longer fit in the lap of the sage.

The mouse-cat-dog-tiger stood taller and thought with gathering rage, "I will go to the sage and maul him! Yes! That is what I will do. It'll show everyone that he no longer controls me. People will no longer think I am a mouse turned into a tiger. They will KNOW I am a real tiger ... as dangerous as any other tiger. They will realize who I am. They will fear and respect me."

The tiger knew where he would find the sage. Without thinking any further, he rushed at the sage and gave a mighty roar. Rishi Muni was in deep meditation and was rudely jolted awake by an angry tiger, crouching, ready to pounce on him.

Startled and then quickly assessing the situation, the yogi raised his hand and zapped the tiger. "You've turned against me?" he shouted, as he turned the magnificent tiger back into a mouse, with just one quick flick of his wrist and one word.

There lay the same mouse that had fallen from the sky, not too many moons ago. The yogi and the mouse regarded each other for a minute. The mouse was crestfallen. The yogi rose, telling the mouse gently, "Take care of yourself, little one." Then, he walked away.

The mouse learnt an important lesson that day – no matter how powerful you become, it is important to stay humble or someone may cut you down to size.

The stories in this collection are adapted from the following Amar Chitra Katha comics:

The Annoying Ant

THE ANNOYING ANT
Script: Cheryl Rao
Art: Sanjhiya Mayekar

THE GHOST THAT GOT AWAY
Script: Aditi Pasumarthy
Art: Dilip Kadam

A Couple of Misers

THE UNWANTED GUEST
Script: Aditi Pasumarthy
Art: Harsho Mohan Chattoraj

The Fearless Boy

THE FEARLESS BOY
Script: Luis M Fernandes
Art: Souren Roy

THE GREAT ARCHITECT
Script: Luis M Fernandes
Art: Souren Roy

The Unhappy Tiger

THE UNHAPPY TIGER
Script: Luis Fernandes
Art: Arjit Dutta Chowdhury

THE AMAR CHITRA KATHA CHAPTER BOOK SERIES

India's rich tapestry is woven together by her stories. These tales can be from the great epics and mythology, or from the ancient history of this rich land. But sometimes the stories of the people, passed down from generation to generation – told at bedtimes and celebrations, in schools and homes – are the most astounding. These are the stories that are part of the great collective inheritance from our past generations.

The Amar Chitra Katha chapter book series brings together some of the greatest tales in the Amar Chitra Katha catalogue. These stories are a celebration of the great collective inheritance from our past generations and aim to bring the reader closer to the thoughts and traditions that make up our country's identity.

The first set in the series, Amar Chitra Katha Folktales Collection, includes *Buddhist Stories*, *Tales of Wit and Wisdom* and *Funny Folktales*.

The second set in the series, Timeless Classics From Amar Chitra Katha, includes *Amazing Folktales*, *Fascinating Stories* and *Unusual Fables*.

The third set in the series, Most Loved Amar Chitra Katha Stories, includes *Jataka Tales*, *Fabulous Fables from India* and *Witty Minister Stories*.

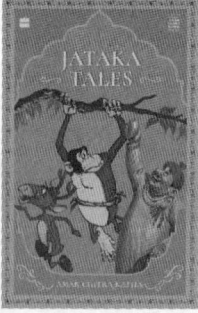

ABOUT ACK

Amar Chitra Katha was founded in 1967 and is a household name in India. It is synonymous with the visual reinvention of the quintessentially Indian stories from the great epics, mythology, history, literature, oral folktales and many other sources.

With a heavy bent on authenticity and meticulous research, Amar Chitra Katha prides itself on being the most informative and trusted storyteller for children. The stories in this series have been adapted directly from the comics for young readers.

Today, Amar Chitra Katha is a cultural phenomenon, custodian of more than 400 comics in 20+ languages that have sold 100+ million copies to date. Amar Chitra Katha is available in bookstores, online and across digital platforms.